The
Forgetful
Wishing Well

Some other books by X. J. KENNEDY

The Owlstone Crown
(A MARGARET K. MC ELDERRY BOOK)

Did Adam Name the Vineagarroon?

Knock at a Star:
A Child's Introduction to Poetry
(with Dorothy M. Kennedy)

The Phantom Ice Cream Man
(A MARGARET K. MC ELDERRY BOOK)

One Winter Night in August
(A MARGARET K. MC ELDERRY BOOK)

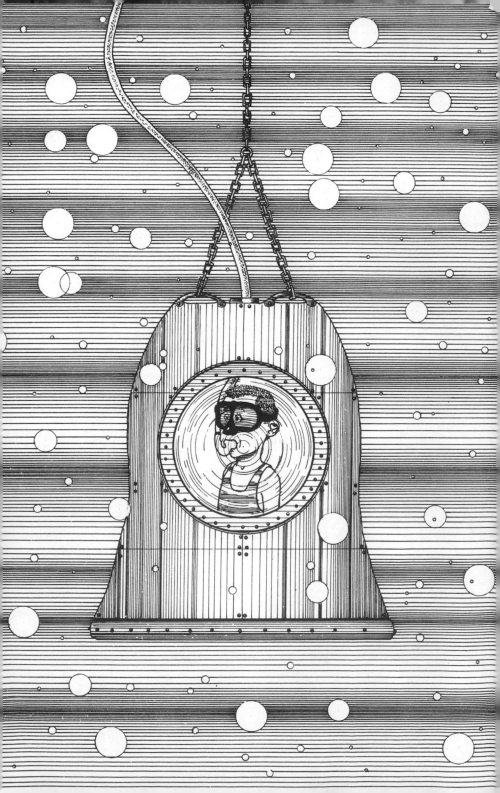

The
Forgetful
Wishing Well

POEMS FOR YOUNG PEOPLE

X. J. Kennedy

with illustrations by Monica Incisa

A MARGARET K. MC ELDERRY BOOK

ATHENEUM   1985   NEW YORK

Library of Congress Cataloging in Publication Data

Kennedy, X. J.
    The forgetful wishing well.

    "A Margaret K. McElderry book."
    Summary: Seventy poems deal with the challenges of
growing up, curious beasts and birds, city life, and other
subjects both realistic and fanciful.
        1. Children's poetry, American. [1. American poetry]
I. Incisa, Monica, ill. II. Title.
    PS3521.E563F6 1985   811'.54   84-45977
    ISBN 0-689-50317-2

Text copyright © 1985 by X. J. Kennedy
Illustrations copyright © 1985 by Monica Incisa
All rights reserved
Published simultaneously in Canada by McClelland & Stewart, Ltd.
Composition by Maryland Linotype Composition
Baltimore, Maryland
Printed and Bound by Fairfield Graphics
Fairfield, Pennsylvania
First Edition

Acknowledgments

    Some of these poems first appeared in the following
books and magazines. The author wishes to thank their editors
and publishers.
    Cricket, the magazine for children: for "A Different
Door," "Spring Storm," and "To a Forgetful Wishing Well."
    Occurrence: for "Where Will We Run to."
    Christmas Poems, selected by Myra Cohn Livingston
(Holiday House): for "Christmas Kaleidoscope."
    The New York Kid's Book, compiled by the Children's
Writers and Artists Collaborative (Doubleday and Company):
for "Forty-seventh Street Crash" and "Flying Uptown Backwards."
    Nude Descending a Staircase by X. J. Kennedy (Doubleday
and Company): for "The Man with the Tan Hands."

For JUDITH McCONNELL,
friend of children's books, friend of children

Contents

PEOPLE I KNOW

FAMILY MATTERS

WONDERS

IN THE CITY

ALL AROUND THE YEAR

Growing Pains

Mixed-up Kid

My brother, learning how to dress,
Puts pants on hindside-to,
Stuffs right foot in his left-foot sock,
Jams left foot in right shoe.

He talks up so he can't be heard,
He pipes down in a shout.
I'll like him better when he gets
Directions figured out.

Girl Who's Moved Around

One time I knew a real good boy,
But that was back in Illinois.

Samantha, she was friends with me,
In Maine—or was it Tennessee?

My father's had six better jobs.
The boys where we live now—what slobs!

They think it's fun to sneak up near
Your ear and yell like mad. I'll cheer

If Father ever sets down foot
Where kids are OK, and stays put.

Trying to Write Thank-You Letters

I'd like to thank you. But I feel
Stuck against something hard and round—
Sort of an orange that won't peel

No matter where I poke my thumb.
I turn my feelings round and round.
The trick is to make the first peel come.

Art Class

Ms. Beecher said I don't know how
   To make a lifelike tree.
Well, all I did was look and draw
   How branches looked to me.

I *know* what you're supposed to do—
   You make a Y, and sitting
On both its arms another two
   Y's. Make them go on splitting.

I went and looked up at a bough
   With bark like scraped black leather,
And neither does a tree know how
   To fit a tree together.

Maturity

I take my plastic rocket ship
To bed, now that I'm older.
My wooly bear is packed away—
Why do the nights feel colder?

Television Nose

"Great balls of fire, Amanda Rose!"
Says Father. "I expect your nose
To grow fast to that TV set—
Why don't you move back farther yet?
What is it with you kids today?
Now run along outside and play!"

I go. But when he's sound asleep
I'll put my bat cape on and creep
Downstairs and switch the TV on
And twist it brighter than the sun
To watch the poorest junk that glows,
With fastened, fascinated nose.

A Quick Hush

I knocked the green alarm clock
Quiet when I threw
It at the wall. Its yammer
Gurgled off. Springs flew
In spirals out of its navel.
Why fling it?
           Well, it shook
Cold morning in my face
And yiped and yiped and yiped:
Wake up! Up! Up! Up! Up!

Creatures

Owl

The diet of the owl is not
   For delicate digestions.
He goes out on a limb to hoot
   Unanswerable questions.

And just because he preens like men
   Who utter grave advice,
We think him full of wisdom when
   He's only full of mice.

A Different Door

When rain falls gray and unabating
And long kept in he stares out waiting
And no one heeds and starts unlatching
Our back door, Tom tries front-door scratching.

That cat, he's not what I'd call bright,
But for a chance—oh, even slight—
Of clearing skies a lark might soar,
Who wouldn't scratch a different door?

Catsnest

Tread.

Tread.

Our cat treads my bed,
Pushing my spread to a heap for his sleep,
Punching sheets, stretching his tailbone up tall.
That it's me underneath doesn't matter at all.

And at last when he's hollowed a hollow he likes
He fits down inside it and, satisfied, purrs
Until Grandmother comes in to turn out my light
And to tell me good night. Then he angrily stirs
And he fluffs up gigantic and glowers, to say:
Well, I did all that digging—why shouldn't *I stay?*

Mole

A point-nosed half-pint parcel, eyes
Pinpoints that hardly twinkle,
He tunnels underneath your lawn
To shoulder up a wrinkle.

Old-Timer

When footsteps go by in the dark
Our slow old hound forgets to bark.

Why, yesterday when Wilsons' cat
Tongue-kissed his nose, he just lay flat.

He'll seldom even bark or stand
And snarl unless some stranger's hand

Approaches with a friendly touch.
At watching he's *some* good. Not much.

Dad knows a man who takes away
Old worn-out dogs. Not ours. He'll stay

Curled in the closet's empty space
And sleep, and dream, and show his face.

Close Call

Across the highway, low and slow,
  Glides reckless robin—car
Slams on its brakes and misses, though
  By no more than as far

As matador feels horn graze cape,
  As skater on thin ice
Skims doom, as gamblers just escape
  With last dimes, shooting dice.

Bat

All day bats drowse in houses' eaves
   Like tents collapsed for storage,
But when dusk darkens, like fall leaves,
   They loosen. Then they forage

For juicy June bugs, meaty moths,
   Mosquitoes (eaten rare).
They're scary. But there's nothing like
   A bat to clear the air.

Future Hero

Out cropping grass, the charcoal-speckled colt,
    Son of Majestic Prince by Golden Dame,
Flicks mane, kicks hoofs, and whinnies in revolt.
    Oh, soon enough they'll saddle him with fame.

One day he'll cross a finish-line—to cheers—
    And there he'll glow, inside our picture tube,
A winner's wreath of roses round his ears.
    Today he makes friends for a sugar cube.

Ant

An ant works hard
Hauling great weight
In our back yard,

But you can't
Hear an ant
Pant.

I *Answer an S.O.S.*

One day in swimming, who should I
Meet but a drowning dragonfly.
White bubbles—tiny bulging moons—
Under his wings clung like pontoons
Or driftwood a drowning man might grasp
To boost him up for one last gasp.
But now so low on hope he was,
He hardly made the softest buzz
Till, cupping him in my right hand,
I set him safe down on dry sand.
Hot sun blazed out and warmed him there—
Then, all undrowned, he took the air,
Circled a breeze, and slowly banked.

It wasn't much. Still, I felt thanked.

Ten Billion Crows

Ten billion crows with cracking bills
Ate all the corn off our eight hills.

Then round and round the sky they soared
And crowed and cruised, and snoozed and snored.

Dad said, "Well, that's the way it goes,
All that fine corn inside those crows."

I hope their bellies ache for weeks.
I hope they crash and break their beaks.

Hummingbird

Cried a scientist watching this creature dart by,
"Why, its wings are too small for it! How dare it fly?"

So he figured and figured and finally found
That it just couldn't possibly get off the ground,

And they made him Professor. But still, hummingbird
Kept on flying to flowerbeds. It hadn't heard.

An Awful Moment

Soon as Caesar, our dog, spied that fox-fur scarf
He jumped to his feet and he started in to arf

And the lady went *Aaaggghhh!* Why, he shot up and took it
Off from around her neck and just shook the thing and shook it.

Dad talked to him a long time. But me, I'm afraid he
Had better steer clear of that hopping mad lady.

She should keep her old scarf out of sight in a box.
Why does one skinny neck need a whole furry fox?

Cat and Wind

Cat watched Wind cross tall grass.
   A mouse, he thought it,
Such as no true cat could let pass.
   With one pounce, caught it,

Lazily spun it. *What to do?*
   How can it fill me?
It's thin enough to see right through.
   Wind shrieked: Don't kill me!

Sweet cat, said Wind, let me go—
   I'll let you tame me.
Nights while you yowl I will yowl too.
   People will blame me.

In June, over your bowl of milk
   I'll breathe cool murmurs,
Blow you smooth notes of silk
   Like some snake-charmer's.

Now, said Cat, *I must dine.*
   Wind, hair abristle,
Darted through cat's paws, clean
   As a wind-whistle.

Wind dwindled out of view.
   Cat, feeling thinner,
Sped home to make sad mew
   Till down came dinner.

People I Know

Mickey Jones

When Mickey Jones
Eats ice cream cones
He gets himself so sticky,

It's never known
Which one is cone
And which is only Mickey.

Wilburforce Fong

Wilburforce Fong,
Wilburforce Fong,
I used to call you funny
But I was wrong.

In school you and I
Would sit down to munch
And you brought (I thought) the funniest
Brown bag lunch.

But now I would trade
The North and South Pole
And all of my brownie
For your great egg roll!

Agnes Snaggletooth

I don't like Agnes Snaggletooth.
How can I ever face her?
Why doesn't the Mafia rub her out
With a Snaggletooth-eraser?

I ape her grin behind her back.
I slide where she just slid.
I'd play with her, but she won't ask.
Well, I wouldn't if she did.

Why don't any *decent* kids move in?
This neighborhood's unlucky.
It's—who's that coming up our walk?
Not *her!* Oh, not that yukky—

Why, Agnes Sneedecker, you rang?
I didn't look for *you.*
Come out and play? Well I don't know.
Live here? I guess I do.

Who, me? *Me* help pull your loose tooth?
And try your racing bike?
Why, Agnes Snag—why, who'd have thought—
Sure. Come in if you like.

Teacher

My teacher looked at me and frowned
A look that must have weighed a pound

And said: When I was young as you
There were some things I did not do.

Elijah Snow

When Elijah Snow
Steps out of his freezer
To sell you a fish
He's one odd-looking geezer:

White icicles hang
From brows stiff as starch
Like the edge of a roof
On the first of March.

From his frozen fur coat
To his boots, he creaks
As though he'd stayed in
With his fish for weeks.

Then he wraps you a codfish
And off you go
Charcoal-warm from a grin
From Elijah Snow.

Family Matters

Muddy Sneakers

Muddy sneakers, make 'em clean—
Throw 'em in the washing machine!
Bucket of soap and a box of starch
And round the dryer hear 'em march!

Held in Suspense

To let Father vacuum the rug under her chair
   Mother—"Oh, do you have to?"—has to raise
Both legs, weary from work, high in the air.
   Like a hungry hound the vacuum cleaner bays.

What a long time he has her hold them up!—
   "Oof! Can't I put them down?" He zips and zaps,
Destroying dust. And Mother, with a deep
   Sigh of relief, at last gets to collapse.

Trying to Make Time on a Country Highway

A yellow leaf blew from a pickup truck
Behind which for seventeen miles we'd been stuck.
The drivers? A couple not far from their graves.
On their bumper sticker it said JESUS SAVES.

Dad was keeping his shoe-sole a steady goad
On the gas through Vermont till by those two slowed
To a neck-and-neck pace with a brook. No mistake,
They had taken much in and had more yet to take.

Like the one crooked link in a playing-out chain,
We kept edging on out toward the left-hand lane,
Getting blocked—dropping back—till we gave up and fell
Into line behind them.

                  And then the spell
Of that slowly unraveling yellow stripe broke,
And our eyes rose high and a colored-up oak
Strode open-armed out, all scurry and sound,
That we'd thought dead wood to be gunned around,
And a lake gazed back and kindled a glow
That had been just a bucket of H_2O.

Unpopular Rex

When our hound dog Rex
   Picked a fight with a skunk
It took ten weeks
   Till his atmosphere shrunk.

All that terrible while,
   Drooping tail, he fretted.
Why do they yell, he wondered,
   When I want to be petted?

House Noises

My mother's big on little fears.
When darkness falls, she sharpens ears:

Outside—who gave that awful shriek?
The storm door that the wind makes creak.

Now what was that? That scraping sound?
Only a leaf blown over ground.

What scurried in the attic? Mice?
The sliding-off-the-roof of ice.

At the back door—did someone cough?
No, but our drainpipe just dropped off.

Porcupine Pa

Whenever Pa neglects to shave
He goes around and kisses
Us loved ones, scratching with his chin—
We duck and hope he misses.

Maybe I lucked out in a way
To get a loving pater,
And yet—who likes to feel like cheese
That's up against a grater?

How to Stay up Late

At night when grown-ups start to yawn
Beneath their reading lamps
Is when I whip my album out
To stick in foreign stamps.

And when pajama time draws near
I start to write the story
Of Lincoln's life, or set up school
Like Maria Montessori.

So kids, wise up. Unless you like
To go to bed too fast
Just save your most impressive play
Of all day long for last.

Wonders

A Sprung Trap

That latchless window on the bottom floor
Gave in when rattled. Yearning to explore
A house that only dust and spiders kept,
We hoisted sneakered feet and in we stepped.

But something waited. With an iron clang
A triggered mousetrap I stepped next to sprang—
Just missed me. But it made my blood run chill.
In my bad dreams, it keeps exploding still.

Now, those who left it—did they plot to set
That trap for me, or did they just forget?
It makes at best a crooked kind of sense
To go off yourself, but leave a mousetrap tense.

Flashlight

Tucked tight in bed, the day all gone,
I like to click my flashlight on,
Then climb in under with my feet
And shine a moon out through the sheet.

I'll throw a circle on the wall,
Move close up to it, make it small,
And then yank back and make that moon
Blow up—an instant light-balloon!

Each flashlight battery, slid out,
Looks piglike with a silver snout
And like two pigs parading, they
Need to line up and look one way.

Ben Franklin with a kite and key
Attracted electricity,
But they must not be also-rans
Who put up light in little cans.

Bowling Alley Wonder

Would you believe it? Even I,
   As though a ball of stone were light,
Can roll loud thunder down a road
   And tumble timber left and right!

An Unexplained Ouch

From in back of our couch
   I suddenly heard
A sound like an ouch!
   Had some wandered bird
Found her way indoors
   Till a floor had stunned her?
Well, I fell to all fours,
   Took a look in under.

But nothing looked wrong
   In that spidery dust—
Just a mousetrap along
   On its way to rust,
A hard chunk of cheese
   That a mouse had bitten,
Two petrified bees
   And a mislaid mitten.

Then our grandfather clock,
   Years behind the time,
Stopped its thick tick-talk
   To let go one chime
That circled the room
   With a shattering sound
Like that of a stone
   Water rings surround.

Had I dreamed? Had that wail
   Been no thing at all

But the cry of a nail
   Wearing out in the wall
Or the ghost of a face
   That our house had kept
Singing down in a place
   Only seldom swept?

Well, I wish I could claim
   That I quickly found
(Like some runaway dime)
   What had made that sound,
But I guess it was one of
   Those playful ghosts
Crying *ouch* to make fun of
   Its scared house-hosts.

Lighting a Fire

One quick scratch
Of a kitchen match
And giant flames unzip!

How do they store
So huge a roar
In such a tiny tip?

My Fishbowl Head

My head's a fishbowl full of fish
   Where, making outs and ins
Through coral doors and windows, swish
   The bright ideas' fins.

Some dart in straight lines, some revolve
   Too quickly to be caught.
Sometimes I read, and sprinkle in
   A little food for thought.

Presents from the Flood

Out in back of our house
   Rain water rises
And from out of long grass
   Lifts a few surprises—

A moss-green golf ball
   And a longlost sneaker,
A rubber dog doll
   With a missing squeaker.

If this rain keeps falling
   For—who knows?—a year,
Will more past-recalling
   Lost things appear?

Like a solid pearl bone
   From some monster bird of
Long ago that no one
   Alive ever heard of?

Like a dinosaur, or—chilling
   Past all belief—
A petrified skeleton
   Indian chief

Who will sit, blink, and glare
   From his birchbark canoe:
What has happened? Where am I?
   What gods are you?

Rock Gardener

I used to think that, underground, stones grow
The way potatoes do in Idaho,

And so believing, every time I'd catch
A pebble, digging up my garden patch,

I'd throw it back in with the understanding
It could lie low until it grew worth landing.

Late Night Flight

Invisible and out of sight,
A thing comes winging through the night
   To find out who's awake in town
And whose roof calls it down to light.

Our house is dark as dark can get
Except one glow: our TV set.
   My babysitter's sound asleep—
It's late. The grown-ups aren't home yet.

And so, for want of other friends,
This weird thing circles and descends
   To touch down on the branches of
Our roof antenna, where it ends

With feathers drooping, wet and spent,
On orders from whoever sent
   It winging through the night to me
Across a moonlit continent.

What is this thing—an eagle? No.
A plane then? No it's not, although
   It carries loads of voice and face
To where I watch, then lets them go.

I'm glad I'm where it has to land
Though now my eyelids droop with sand
   From all its ads for pain-relief,
Decaffeinated coffee, and . . .

Tear

A teardrop in your eye
   To others may look small,
But looked through, it stands high
   As China's thick brick wall.

Sentries

From either side of Wheelers' walk
 They stand and stare all year,
Those stiff fake beasts I like to stalk,
 That pair of statue-deer.

They must be made of stainless steel.
 At winter's fiercest blow
With icy eyes they'll watch you while
 Their antlers stack with snow.

I wonder what they find to think,
 And do the things they feel
Roll round inside their hollow heads
 Like balls of stainless steel?

Where Will We Run to

Where will we run to
When the moon's
Polluted in its turn

And the sun sits
With its wheels blocked
In the used-star lot?

The Secret Joy of Diving Bells

The secret joy of diving bells
Isn't to hunt for lost gold rubles.
It is just falling, blowing bubbles,
As pails do, tumbling down deep wells.

In the City

Flying Uptown Backwards

Squeezing round a bend, train shrieks
Like chalk on gritty blackboards.

People talk or read or stare.
Street names pass like flashcards.

Hope this train keeps going on
Flying uptown backwards.

The Man with the Tan Hands

The man
With the tan
Hands
Who stands
And scoops
Up
Roast
Chest-
Nuts
In cups
Of old
News
Folded
Like perching
Birds

Sold
Me a few
New
Words.

Forty-Seventh Street Crash

Truck stopped.
Taxi didn't.
Bumper bopped.
Windshield splintered.

JERK! says truck,
Why didn't you stop?
I did, says hack.

Fists whack.

How to Watch Statues

Don't snicker and sneer
And say, What is it?—
Go on, open your eyes.
Let it come visit.

Stationed in stone,
This discus-thrower
Has thrown a long while
And grown no slower.

Here's a strange baboon
That will take you far—
For its skull Picasso
Used an old toy car.

See, you just have to stand
In front of a statue
Until, ready to talk,
It looks right at you.

Boulder, Colorado

Skyscrapers made of earth—stones—trees
Take up as much sky as they please

And deck with white clouds, streams, wild flowers
Their top-floor observation towers.

Roofscape

The sun in white whiskers
Strolls boldly each roof
Ignoring the warning:
EMPLOYEES KEEP OFF.

From far below echo
Trash men bouncing cans
And, windily whirring,
Conditioner fans.

Tanks stuffed full of water—
Fat dragonflies—perch.
A skyscraper shadows
A low-kneeling church.

Trouble in Town

Glass in the gutter.
No street light.
Looks like trouble
In the town tonight.

Cops on every corner.
Storefronts boarded tight.
Siren purring, no one stirring
Round the town tonight.

Hush, you children.
Hug your beds. That's right.
Never mind that crashing.
Just somebody trashing
Down the town tonight.

Valentine

If all the whole world's taxicabs
Came running to my call,
I'd park right by your door and honk
In the handsomest cab of all.

We'd drive to Spain, Maine, or Spokane!
Could anything be sweeter
Than ticking off a million miles
Upon a metal meter?

All Around the Year

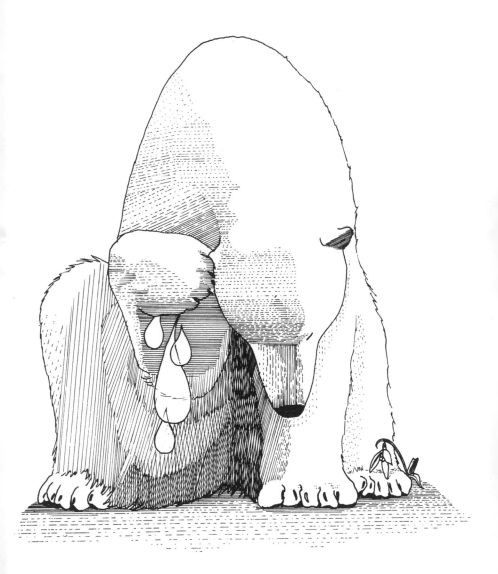

Blow-up

Our cherry tree
Unfolds whole loads
Of pink-white bloom—
It just explodes.

For three short days
Its petals last.
Oh, what a waste.
But what a blast.

First One Out of Bed

Up through the ground,
    Having just awoke,
With a leap and a bound
    Early Crocus broke,

Took a quick look around,
    Shouted: *Holy smoke!*
All the world's sleeping sound!
    Up jumped Artichoke.

Definitions

Fog: a cloud
That no matter how hard it tried
Couldn't get off the ground.

Cloud: a fog
That finally got tired
Lying around, a lot of useless weather.

So now it walks the sky
Trying to bunch a rain-bouquet together.

Rain into River

Rain into river
falling

tingles

one
at
a
time

the trout's
tin shingles.

Summer Milk

In summer, like a breeze at dawn,
Our milkman as a rule
Blows by and leaves six cardboard bricks
Sweet, cloverful, and cool.

The milk! The milk! we scream at noon
And bring in sour quarts
That taste like lukewarm vinegar.
They say it's good for warts.

Two of a Kind

Where I stood still, whirring
   My rod and reel,
The old stone mill stood stirring
   Its slow mill wheel.

Was our luck much? Neither
   That mealy mill's nor mine.
It reeled in its river,
   I reeled in line.

My Window Screen

My window screen, all crisscrossed wire,
Has half a million eyes,
Each big enough to let in air
But baffle summer flies.

Mosquito comes, he bumps his head——
My screen won't open wide.
All night it strains between my bed
And all there is outside.

Pick Your Own

Where gates say PICK YOUR OWN, and trees
  With tons of round red apples sag,
You pick as much as you can squeeze
  Inside a four-quart paper bag.

Some pickers know how not to spill—
  They stop in time and add no more,
But I come staggering back downhill
  With the ones too beautiful to ignore.

How can those careful quitters stand
  To leave so much and not look back
And, all that ripe red fruit at hand,
  Take home one empty inch of sack?

Brooms

When pigeons clutter up July
    A warm whisk broom of breeze
Gently collects them from the sky
    And settles them in trees.

Then in comes, on Fall cleaning-day,
    To drive the dry unpinned
Leaf litter whooshing on its way,
    A brisk push broom of wind.

To a Forgetful Wishing Well

All summer long, your round stone eardrum held
Wishes I whispered down you. None came true.
Didn't they make one ripple in your mind?
I even wished a silver pail for you.

Sleepy Schoolbus

Weekends, the battered yellow bus
    That calls at all our houses
And honks its horn to hurry us
    Draws shut its doors and drowses

Till, roused by Monday lunchbox smells,
    It yawns and reappears.
You look all worn out, yellow bus.
    Go home. Doze ten more years.

Halloween Disguises

Something's come over pumpkins.
    They're not themselves.
Those innocent bumpkins
    Seem changed to wolves.
Now a flickering flame
    To each shell arrives
And they bare zigzag fangs
    Thanks to paring knives.

Even kind Constance Bunting,
    Gray-haired, grand-maternal,
Into paper napkins counting
    Each candy corn kernel
As she lovingly plans
    Trick-or-treat donations
Seems a witch who intones
    Evil incantations.

Even commonplace cats
    Of familiar mew
Look outlandish as wizards
    From Katmandu,
Who with magic-wand tails,
    Yellow eyes appalling,
Greet the round moon with wails
    And caterwauling.

Moonwalk

Snow kept on sifting through the night,
Now all of earth today
Is one wide moon for me to walk—
Whatever will I weigh?

I want to take a giant step!
Quick, snap my snowsuit snappers!
A moon with not one footprint yet
And no one's candy wrappers!

Christmas Kaleidoscope

Chuck-full boxes, packages——
   squeeze 'em, feel sharp angles!
     From candy-caned
     evergreen
      a tinfoil
      rainfall
         dangles.

Cold-tongued bells are tolling,
   tolling, *Hark, the herald*
     angels sing
     Christ the King!
      Earth's
      rebirth
         is caroled.

Sheep and ox guard manger,
   Magi offer gifts.
     Down through white
     silent night
      slow
      snow
         sifts.

Spring Storm

Our old fat tiger cat
With no claw on one toe
Prints four-leaf clovers in
The sneaky April snow,

The sneaky April snow that sprang
As quiet as a cat
Down on our budding apple tree
And bashed its branches flat

And made me cry a little bit.
Get gone now, sneaky snow.
Come in, soft grass, come stealing in
With no claw on one toe.

All Around the Year

Now Winter, that mean polar bear,
Goes loping back inside its lair
And lets a river, melting, tug
Loose of its terrible bear hug.

With tree roots now, earth starts to seethe.
Now early shoots peer forth to breathe.
Now willow branches will grow high
And so will I. And so will I.